Nine Steps to Becoming a Transition Entrepreneur

From Employee to Entrepreneur

J. BILAL

First Edition

authorHOUSE®

AuthorHouse™
1663 Liberty Drive
Bloomington, IN 47403
www.authorhouse.com
Phone: 1-800-839-8640

© 2011 by J. Bilal. All rights reserved.

No part of this book may be reproduced, stored in a retrieval system, or transmitted by any means without the written permission of the author.

Published by AuthorHouse 12/29/2011

ISBN: 978-1-4685-2364-5 (sc)
ISBN: 978-1-4685-2362-1 (e)
ISBN: 978-1-4685-2363-8 (dj)

Library of Congress Control Number: 2011962505

Any people depicted in stock imagery provided by Thinkstock are models, and such images are being used for illustrative purposes only.
Certain stock imagery © Thinkstock.

This book is printed on acid-free paper.

Because of the dynamic nature of the Internet, any web addresses or links contained in this book may have changed since publication and may no longer be valid. The views expressed in this work are solely those of the author and do not necessarily reflect the views of the publisher, and the publisher hereby disclaims any responsibility for them.

CONTENTS

SELF-DISCOVERY

Step One Define Yourself	3
Step Two Make the Connections	25
Step Three Center of Gravity	37

CREATE YOUR BRIDGE

Step Four Business Research	49
Step Five Build Your Business Brand	57
Step Six Network Marketing Plan	63

THE TRANSITION

Step Seven Business Plan Format	71
Step Eight Investment Strategy	75
Step Nine Initiate the Business	81

AFTERWORD

Foreword

The business world has changed significantly over the last decade. Many major corporations have failed, merged, or restructured. In the process, many unskilled and skilled workers, including professionals, have been, downsized, and left to their own resources without employment.

For the many capable people unable to find work, the need for guidance and direction is greater than ever now. The future of our global economy depends upon working citizens and healthy business communities—it all begins and ends with people. Every day, citizens are searching for new ways to sustain and enhance their livelihood but are finding few options.

J.Bilal advocates for unskilled workers' and working professionals' opportunities to build a personal enterprise. He is a motivational and strategic thinker who understands the importance of empowering others to control their professional destiny.

Read this book to discover how you can make the transition from completely dependent employee to empowered entrepreneur. This book will teach you commonsense yet powerful concepts that will open your mind to a new reality, inspiring you to think, reflect, and discuss your new understandings within your circle of influence. This book is intended to be both informational and actionable, a tool to help you build a profitable business. . It's about you making a fully informed choice, a choice that serves a greater purpose than the one you have today as an employee.

Acknowledgments

Special thanks to Warna Abdullah, Theresa Lovelady, John M. Brown, Tarvella Razi, Damien Haitsuka, Marcellus Rainey, Bob Marshall for your guidance. Thank you to my dear friends and family for your unconditional love and support.

Message from the Author

The time has come for you to fully explore what is possible beyond being an employee. There are many fears and risks that come with stepping out on your own to start a new business. I know this personally; I, too, felt those emotions before I became a transition entrepreneur. For most people who have worked at one job the majority of their career, entrepreneurship is the riskiest proposition they will ever consider. Typically their fear lies in the ultimate risk of losing the financial rewards, benefits, and personal satisfaction that come from having a stable career or solid job. Today, however, the assurance of long-term employment with the same company with job security has become rare to nonexistent. Furthermore, the quality of your employment experience can vary along with the never-ending changes in a company's management, leadership, philosophy, and strategy.

I am providing you with an opportunity to look into

yourself to find the rewards and benefits you expect. This book outlines a practical, nine-step process for exploring this opportunity while minimizing some of the fears many face as they seek to become independent business owners.

Thank you for investing your valuable time and resources to allow me to share this process and my concepts with you. I am confident that the time you will spend reading and the money you have invested will be well worth the experience.

J.Bilal

Self-Discovery

"Happiness depends upon ourselves."

Aristotle

Step One
Define Yourself

Do you have thoughts about how it would feel to be your own boss? Do you then dismiss those thoughts, fearing the risks involved? Reality check: as an employee, you already risk losing your job today. Imagine your boss calling you into the office, presenting you with your last paycheck, or escorting you from the building. How would you support yourself, pay your bills, feed your family, maintain your lifestyle? Furthermore, what would you lose in terms of dignity and self-worth, or respect and reputation within your community?

Defined in its most literal sense, an employee is a person who works for another in return for financial or other compensation. How well does the word *employee* define you? That identity is suitable for many happy and hardworking citizens; it may be a perfect fit—today. But what does the future hold? In this first chapter we will explore whether or not you wish to accept that identity for the long term.

Becoming an entrepreneur is the polar opposite of being an employee; an entrepreneur is someone who assumes risk for a business enterprise. A *transition entrepreneur* is someone who transfers his or her value as an employee into an independent business as an owner. This transition is done seamlessly over time while maintaining consistent employment. Such a transition takes patience and personal sacrifice and investment.

There are intrinsic and material reasons for becoming a transition entrepreneur. I propose to you that by doing so, you can gain a higher level of self-actualization, unlimited earning capacity, and more freedom to create a personal legacy. If you agree, you may be ready to take the leap of faith and become part of a very special group. To get there, however, we will need to take a journey together through the three important sections of this book:

1. You will rediscover who you are by further defining yourself beyond the context of *employee*.
2. You will learn how to create a career bridge for your business opportunity through effective research.

3. You will design a transition business plan that will help you arrive at your destination of becoming a transition entrepreneur.

Self-Actualization

Defining yourself begins with understanding what you need and what motivates you. We all have needs and are driven to act based on our motivations. Let's apply this basic principle to how we evaluate ourselves as employees.

Skilled workers and working professionals are often defined by their job or their earnings, and those earnings typically shape their social status. We are motivated to work by the type of lifestyle we believe we need.

To take a deeper look at the dynamics of human motivation, let's draw upon the classic psychological concept developed by Dr. Abraham Maslow.

Maslow's Hierarchy of Needs

1. **Physiological needs:** all biological needs including food, water, and oxygen
2. **Safety needs:** shelter, public security, health coverage, and safe environmental conditions
3. **Social needs:** love, affection, and

relationships of all types—platonic, romantic, and familial

4. **Self-Esteem needs:** self-respect, respect from others, self-worth, and recognition for accomplishments

5. **Self-Actualization:** self-awareness, fulfillment of full potential, and the realization of one's passion or purpose in life

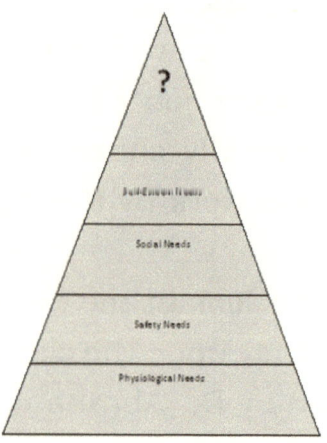

Figure 1.1 Maslow's Hierarchy of Needs

The benefits of the top motivation level, self-actualization, can only be attained by fulfilling the four lower levels, and fulfilling those lower-level needs is often enough for one to have satisfaction in life. In most cases, stable employment and income can enable a person to fulfill those lower motivations.

Ironically, your employment situation can potentially inhibit your ability to attain self-actualization.

The process of reaching self-actualization is the first and most important variable in the transition entrepreneur equation, and it is the one that most people struggle with as employees. Self-actualization is important and highly underrated in the hierarchy of needs. It is often confused with self-esteem; therefore, few people seek to achieve it. We are going to address the mysterious human need to attain self-actualization, removing the question mark from your pyramid and replacing it with your answer.

Imagine living with a sense of enjoyment and purpose that you've created on your terms. Visualize the empowerment you can gain from being your fully creative self and feeding your passion through what you do every day. As a transition entrepreneur, you will have a higher probability of attaining self-actualization on your own terms. The rights, risks, and rewards of owning your own business come with a self-understanding beyond the bounds of a job description created by an employer.

Having been a hardworking employee, I must note that many employees are fully satisfied with that position; many are working in great careers or fulfilling job assignments for well-regarded employers. There are obviously millions of employees who earn reasonable compensation and fringe benefits and, as a result, feel some level of job security. I speak from experience when I say it is perfectly feasible for an employee to earn respect, merit, and recognition from an employer; still, that does not guarantee self-actualization, a sense of purposefulness, fulfillment of passion, and creative freedom.

As an employee, is this position where you begin or end? Who owns and has rights to all the work and time you have invested in your experience, training, education, and professional relationships—you or your employer? If you believe that you have potential beyond your current job or career, you may be on the verge of making a powerful and motivated step towards becoming something more than just an employee. Take a moment to think about and write down answers to the following questions. (I would recommend that you use a notepad or journal that you can reference as a working document of your learning experiences with this book.)

What are your talents and passions?

What is your potential to grow and learn in your current role?

Your answers to these questions will help you with the gap assessment exercise later in this chapter. A gap assessment measures where you are versus where you aspire to be. After you have written down your answers, therefore, set them aside; you will revisit them at the end of this chapter.

Financial Wealth

Now let's build upon our first conversation about self-actualization by discussing what can be an uncomfortable and perplexing topic: financial wealth. Employees work to earn a personal income, and that income is a form of power. Your current financial position is likely tied to your earned income. An employee's earned income and future earning capacity are determined by his or her job performance and by the process by which his or her employer evaluates that performance. Pay raises and bonuses driven by performance evaluations are controlled by the employer compensation process. Therefore most working professionals depend completely upon this process to achieve or maintain their desired lifestyle. Now that we've established these fundamentals, let's delve into the importance of financial wealth.

What are financial resources? They might include current earned income as well as past earned income in the form of cash on reserve and capital assets that can be readily converted into cash.

Your wealth is the sum of your financial resources and your material possessions that have market value. The market value of those possessions varies according to the type of assets and the market conditions. Furthermore, what you consider to be valuable resources may be less valuable to your co-worker or neighbor. Therefore, your position of wealth can vary daily by the market valuation and opinions of potential buyers.

Your economic wealth is the *net worth* of your total assets less total liabilities. If you add all your tangible resources (land, property, and capital) and your financial resources (cash reserves, stocks, bonds, business equity, and total capital investments) and subtract all your liabilities (loans, revolving credit balances, and other debts), you arrive at a numerical net worth. See the following example.

Table 1.1 Net Worth (Assets)

Asset	Type	Value
Home	Real Estate	$200,000
Retirement Fund	Stocks/Bonds	$150,000
Personal Savings	Cash	$10,000
Total Assets		**$360,000**

Table 1.2 Net Worth (Liabilities)

Liabilities	Type	Debt
Home Mortgage	Loan	$125,000
Student Loan	Loan	$15,000
Credit Cards	Revolving Credit	$10,000
Total Liabilities		**$150,000**

In this simple example, the net worth is calculated

by subtracting the total liabilities from the total assets: $360,000 - $150,000 = $210,000 (net worth). This is a *positive net worth* of $210,000, which is favorable. In some instances, however, hardworking individuals come to the unfortunate realization that they have a *negative net worth*. That happens when the total liabilities (what you owe) exceed the total assets (what you own). An employee with a positive net worth has a favorable financial exit strategy in the case of unexpected loss of employment. But whether an employee has a positive or a negative net worth, it is risky for him or her to rely solely on an employer to determine his or her future financial wealth.

Before you continue reading, take a moment to calculate your current net worth. List all your assets, as in Table 1.1. Next, list all your liabilities, as in Table 1.2. Use a calculator to total your assets and liabilities and then subtract your total liabilities from your total assets to determine your current net worth.

Your net worth is what you have to fall back on if you were to find yourself without a steady source of income tomorrow. The type of assets you possess could be easy or difficult to convert to cash quickly. Remember, cash is king—it's the fastest way to replace your income. Understanding your net worth should help you think about your personal income differently, as conditional and not constant. Many employees feel secure with just their income, their current savings, and their assets—until the income stops coming in. Your income could end tomorrow if you find yourself unemployed.

You have seen a simple example of how to calculate wealth in the form of net worth, and you have completed your own calculation to see where you stand. Now it is time to do some soul-searching about your current position. Answer the following questions:

How much financial wealth do you need to attain your lifestyle?

What will it take in terms of job performance and earnings to reach your life goals?

These questions are provocative by intent, and again, your answers will be part of the upcoming gap assessment exercise. Take some time now to write down your answers in your notepad or journal.

It is important to expand the scope of our discussion about wealth. The distribution of wealth among employees and business owners in the United States reveals a lot about the potential winners and losers in our economy. The statistics that follow and a simple illustration of wealth distribution (Chart 1.1) will explain my point. Then we will discuss common ways to acquire wealth and the power that comes with it.

First, let's point out the painfully obvious: the distribution of wealth in the United States is imbalanced, favoring the wealthiest 20 percent of Americans.

- The wealthiest 1 percent of Americans owns 35 percent of all privately held wealth.
- The next 19 percent owns 50 percent of all privately held wealth.
- That leaves the remaining 15 percent of wealth to be shared by the bottom 80 percent of the American population, as blue collar and white collar employees scrap for that small slice of the economic pie.

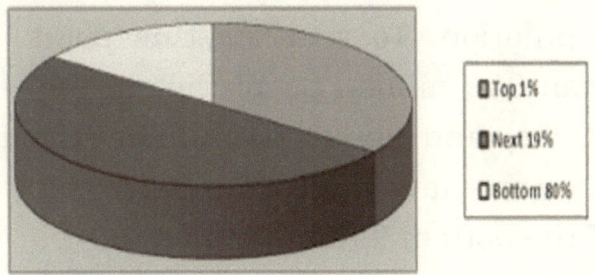

U.S. Wealth Distribution – Chart 1.1

- The top wealthiest 20 percent of American citizens have accumulated or received their wealth over time. This wealth is concentrated in the following financial buckets: business equity, financial securities (e.g., stocks, bonds, mutual funds, and non-residential real estate). These sorts of assets are high-return, *unearned*-income-producing resources. The income gained from these assets significantly reduces the need for the wealthiest citizens to work to produce earned income. These citizens don't depend on an employer to maintain or expand their lifestyles. The income gained from these high-return assets also empowers the wealthy to minimize their use of credit (liabilities) in order to expand their spending power. The net effect of this imbalance in American wealth distribution is that the wealthiest likely will own the largest percentage of wealth as a minority within the overall population. To reiterate this point: more than 300 million people live in the United States, and about 30 million—the top 1 percent—have more than twice the wealth of the bottom 240 million.

I know what you are asking yourself right now: *How do I move into the top 1 or 20 percent tier?* I'll answer with another question, which will offer some perspective and further support my argument for becoming a transition entrepreneur:

How did the wealthy get wealthy?

Did they earn it by working more overtime at their day job? Did they work two jobs to accelerate their earning capacity? Did they climb the company ladder overnight by making friends with all the right people? The answer to all these questions is a resounding no. Knowing that should help you be realistic and accept that you will need to acquire more wealth on your own terms. Move beyond the limitations of acquiring wealth as an employee.

Now that you have completed a calculation of your net worth, you can determine if you are where you need to be now or where you want to be in the future. Remember, it is not your employer's responsibility or objective to ensure that you achieve your financial goals. It is up to you to expand your wealth beyond the reach of your personal earned income. I propose that the opportunity of reaching your financial goals can best be achieved as a transition entrepreneur.

So how did the wealthy acquire their wealth? The top three ways that wealth is acquired today are through ownership of business equity; significant, high-return capital investments; and inheritance—or a combination of these sources.

Up to 60 percent of the privately held wealth in the United States is acquired through business equity. Owning equity in a profitable business can happen in a variety of ways. You can purchase an existing business, which requires assets; you can invest in a business (stocks), which also requires assets; or you can build a business enterprise, which again requires assets. Note that assets are what drive and deliver wealth, no matter how you cut it.

Some 35 to 39 percent of American wealth is attained through capital investment in financial securities of all types, including stocks, bonds, annuities, and mutual funds. Guess what? That takes assets too! Finally, about 1 percent of the total wealth in the United States is gained through inheritance. So if you do not possess large assets or a large inheritance, own a very profitable business, or have an abundance of successful capital investments, you probably are not among the wealthiest 20 percent of American citizens.

Of the three main ways to attain wealth, the most likely way to do it is by using your assets to build a successful business. Use what you have in the form of human assets (intellectual assets, skill assets) and personal earned income to invest in a business of your own and gain a high return on those assets. Attaining greater self-actualization and expanding your financial wealth as a business owner helps establish your personal legacy as you become a transition entrepreneur.

Personal Legacy

So far we have unlocked the door to understanding the highest level of human motivation using Maslow's Hierarchy of Needs. We have also addressed the cold reality of American economics: the difference between personal earned income and wealth. By discussing net worth and breaking down the distribution of wealth in the United States, we've assessed how you fit into the big picture.

The sum of two powerful variables, **self-actualization** plus expanded **financial wealth,** equals the end result of creating a **personal economic legacy.** This is the core reason to become a transition entrepreneur.

Let's take inventory of what we have explored so far.

Self-Actualization:
Does your career or job fully define who you are and allow you to aspire to greatness?

Financial Wealth:
Does your career or job enable you to maximize your earning capacity and assets to support with your preferred lifestyle?

These questions lead to the first self-defining concept I'll introduce, the **Personal Legacy**

Equation (PLE). This concept proposes that adding the highest motivation level, self-actualization (SA), and unlimited financial wealth (FW) results in a powerful combination to create a (personal legacy (PL).

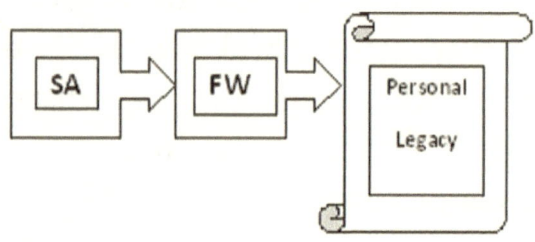

Figure 1.2 – Personal Legacy Equation

Your life purpose, your experiences, and your achievements become the legacy you leave behind. No matter where you go, there you are. Unfortunately, most employees are incomplete and functioning without the sense of purpose that would create a life legacy. As an employee, you should not be surprised by what you lack in motivation, purposefulness, and financial growth. Your role as an employee limits your ability to create a personal legacy.

The two most valuable and sought-after resources are money and time. Not everyone has the same amount of money. However, regardless of our job or career, we all have the same number of hours in a day or a week. Think about how you spend your time; that speaks volumes about your living legacy.

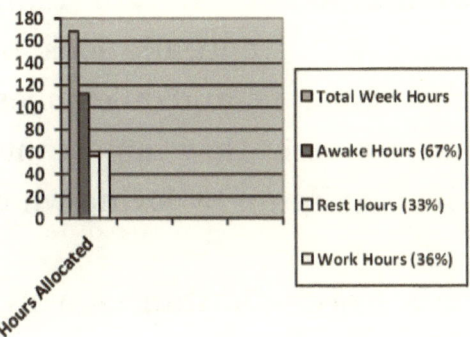

Figure 1.3 - Life Hours Allocation

Most of us spend more than a third of our lives (36 percent of our hours per week) at work. And many of us actually sleep less and work more than the American average, which means we may be overworked and under-rested. Based on these averages, most American workers spend half or more of their waking hours at work. The remaining hours are left over for leisure time and other activities. There are so many physical and mental health implications with this sort of imbalance, including stress, depression, anxiety, obesity, chemical dependency, and loss of all motivation.

It is sobering to think about how we are spending our lives as employees. A third of an employee's life is devoted to work or other career obligations. Time for a gut check, especially if you are a disengaged employee doing something you do not love, working for a company you do not value, or not earning enough to live your preferred lifestyle. You may be wasting your life. Moreover, your family, friends, and community will eventually look back on the events, accomplishments, and milestones of your life to define who you were. How important is it to live your life to the maximum by loving what you do for a living?

Even in the best of circumstances, a highly engaged employee is still one who ultimately contributes only to the company's bottom line. What about your bottom line, your motivation, your future returns in financial wealth that will empower you to live your personal legacy? Becoming a transition entrepreneur means you can reinvest your full potential into your own life to build your personal legacy.

The **gap assessment exercise,** below, is an effective task to help you begin a deeper self exploration. This exercise is going to be your mirror, reflecting your potential to move from employee to business owner.

Gap Assessment Exercise

Purpose:

The gap assessment exercise will require you to put into action what you have learned and explored in this chapter. You will begin by gathering some resources and answering a few questions; then you will complete some tasks to fulfill the exercise. In the end, you will know whether or not you have a gap in your life as an employee that can be filled by becoming a transition entrepreneur.

Resources:
1. Your updated résumé
2. Your current job description with compensation information
3. A journal of your answers to questions and notes from this chapter

Print out your resume and job description. Make sure you have on hand at least two different color highlighters (yellow and green), plus a pen or pencil to take notes.

Questions:
1. What are your talents and passions?
2. What is your potential to grow and learn in your current role?
3. How much financial wealth do you need to attain your preferred lifestyle?
4. What will it take in terms of job performance and earnings to reach your life goals?

This exercise will work only if you are totally honest with yourself. Find a private, quiet place at a desk or table where you will have time alone, without distractions, for up to an hour. Lay out your résumé, job description, a blank notepad or journal page, and this book with the questions in front of you. You are now ready to discover career-altering answers.

Gap Assessment Exercise Steps:

A. Highlight in yellow the tasks in your job description that you enjoy most. Compare what you highlighted with your answers to Question 1.

B. Highlight in yellow your favorite positions on your résumé. Compare what you highlighted with your answers to Question 2.

C. Highlight in green your current salary and bonus opportunities on your job description. Write down your projected salary increase and bonuses for the next twelve months.

D. Compare your projected salary increase and bonus opportunities to what you think you will need to cover your lifestyle expenses for the next twelve months.

E. Write down a dollar figure for how much you want to increase your net worth over the next twelve months. Compare this figure to what you think you can save or invest out of your personal income over that same period of time.

F. Write down any desired promotion or position you hope to attain in your company within the next twelve months. Evaluate whether or not it would provide you more income, be more personally fulfilling, or allow you to further maximize your talents.

The six evaluations (A–F) in this exercise will give you some thinking and talking points to help identify any gaps. Specifically, A and B will help you process the links or gaps between your personal motivation and your growth potential in your current job. The gaps you are looking for are relative to the two variables of the PLE—that is, self-actualization and financial wealth. If your current employment alone does not match up to what you want to achieve in those areas, you may be at risk of never realizing your personal legacy.

Even if you trust yourself to be honest in this exercise, it is not enough to make a full assessment on your own. To complete this assessment, seek out additional input from at least two trusted advocates who will provide you honest, direct feedback; they could include a spouse, friend, colleague, family member, or mentor. Ask each of them to give you an hour of his or her time to discuss your career goals. Open the dialogue with a quick overview of what you have read in this book, followed by what you learned in your gap assessment exercise. Ask your advocates to provide you specific feedback about the perceived links or gaps you have identified.

If possible, meet during the weekend over a meal

or a cup of coffee (your treat) to ensure you have plenty of time, without work conflicts. Be an active listener; take copious notes as you receive feedback from your advocates. Based on the combination of those notes and your notes from the assessment, you should be able to determine the severity of your gaps, and you should be able to answer the questions presented earlier in this chapter:

"How well does the word employee define you? That identity is suitable for many happy and hardworking citizens; it may be a perfect fit—today. But what does the future hold?"

As we've seen, gaps in attaining a higher self-actualization (SA) + gaps in maximizing financial wealth (FW) = significant gaps that limit the creation of a personal legacy (PL). Filling those gaps through the ownership of a profitable and successful business is the logical bridge to creating a personal legacy, part of the process of becoming a transition entrepreneur.

Do you believe in the PLE concept, and are you willing to make the commitment to start your transition? If the answer is yes, the rest of this book will be a valuable journey for you; you will learn a great deal about yourself and your ability to build your own business. As with many journeys, the first step is the most difficult one, because you had to face your biggest challenge: you.

Step Two
Make the Connections

You have completed the gap assessment exercise in the first chapter through introspection and answering meaningful questions. What you have discovered about yourself by exploring the PLE concept is the most important point. Now you are ready to do something different. You're ready to move beyond being simply an employee in order to achieve what is most valuable to everyone, a personal legacy, attained through greater self-actualization and financial wealth.

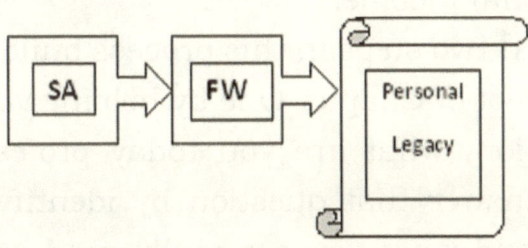

Figure 1.2 – Personal Legacy Equation

PLE: (SA) Self Actualization + (FW) Financial Wealth = (PL) Personal Legacy

As an employee, becoming a transition entrepreneur is the best way for you to fulfill the PLE. The variables in this equation are a no-nonsense and practical way to start creating your personal legacy. This equation process helped you define yourself in one of two ways and make a choice: being an employee is not enough. You also should now know the answer to a fundamental question: why should you become a transition entrepreneur? The simple answer is that you want more than a job, more than a paycheck, and more than the knowledge that you've contributed to your employer's success.

So congratulations—you are on your way to creating your own personal legacy by building your own business. Moreover, you are going to do it in a transitional way that takes advantage of your current situation as an employee, mitigating the risks that many entrepreneurs encounter when they attempt to launch a new business without current employment and personal income.

The next two steps in this process build upon the base concept of Chapter One by helping you answer the question, what are you today professionally? We will answer that question by identifying what you love and what you are really good at doing. It is time for you to pinpoint your passion and your talents without the limitations of a job description or employer evaluation.

Passion

The greatest achievements are driven by personal passion. When you are able to do something you find exciting, there is a natural force that turns work into play. Often we hear successful professional athletes discuss their sport as a child would a fun game. They simply appreciate the privilege of being able to do what they love for a living. This utopian ideal is possible in other professions, too. Put aside the pressures a professional athlete faces to win games and entertain fans; most professional athletes are simply doing what they love and having fun competing. It is conceivable that any professional could have that same experience, the reward of working in a field he or she loves. First, however, that professional must understand his or her own passion.

True passion is an undeniable feeling. It is a burning inside that is consistently on the verge of boiling over, fueled by energy and enthusiasm. It is the feeling that wakes you up in the morning, inspiring you to go and do what you enjoy most. If you experience this every day in your current profession, terrific! But if that passion is being invested into something other than your purpose to build your own personal legacy, it may be wasted or discounted at best.

It's difficult to channel passion if you don't know exactly what you are passionate about. This is a common barrier for many working professionals; their lack of passion or lack of understanding about their personal passion keeps them from making positive career moves or venturing off on their own. If you are not sure where your passions lie, you are on a career journey without a key navigational tool.

Let's leverage the psychoanalytic concept of Dr. Sigmund Freud's "pleasure principle" to create more context around this topic. According to this principle, human beings' rudimentary desire is to pursue pleasure and avoid pain. Freud also suggested that the need to fulfill a desire or passion is not limited by reality (what he referred to as the "reality principle").

To avoid getting too technical, I won't fully define all three of Freud's structural models of the human psyche—id, ego, and superego. However, it is relevant to draw a connection to the first model, the id. This concept of the pleasure principle is supported by the function of the id, the part of the psyche occupied with the need to fulfill desire, pleasure, and passion, without regard for consequences. The "id" state of mind is very much like that of a young child. Watch young children at play long enough, or think back to when you were a child, and you will see that children live fancy-free. Here are some fun examples of the pleasure principle manifested in the behavior of a young child:

- A young boy running freely in a shopping center, lollipop in hand, giggling and causing mischief to attract the attention of others
- A little girl standing in front of her classmates during show-and-tell, rambling aimlessly about every detail of her favorite doll
- Children yelling and screaming with excitement as they play a favorite game for hours on a long summer day, without regard for time

It is curious how we lose a little bit of that "pleasure principle" behavior each day as we grow older and transform into conforming adult employees. Understandably, the childlike behavior described in these examples is not appropriate in the business world. However, the source of that kind of pleasure, desire and passion is essential to success in business.

For many employees, the pendulum has swung to the other extreme; they work at a job that provides little to no pleasure. Imagine, even worse, working a job whose only reward is the income and which does not inspire or draw upon human passion.

Look back on your own childhood and try to recall whether you ever heard a classmate stand up and announce, "I want to grow up and become a modestly compensated, unoriginal, micromanaged, hardworking employee doing something I really am not passionate about for a living." Chances are, that probably didn't happen. But there is a strong possibly that if you look up some of your old friends or classmates and take a poll, you'll find that most of them are living that life now. Sadly, it seems that the time in our lives when we are most honest with ourselves and least afraid to dream big is when we are children.

Dig deep into your inner child, your id, and draw upon Freud's pleasure principle to find your passion as you complete the following **task inventory exercise**. This is a two-part exercise that will help you connect some valuable pieces of information during your journey. Do yourself a favor by being completely honest about your passions. Try not to worry about how outlandish or insignificant they may seem; just focus on what you really enjoy doing. This will be difficult for some and fun and easy for others, depending on their comfort level with self-evaluation.

The **task inventory exercise** will help uncover your passion (P) and start building the first element of a concept I call the **Business Plan Compass (BPC)**. Record the information from this task in your working notepad or journal.

The Business Plan Compass uses passion (P), talent (T), and business opportunity (O) to direct your transition to entrepreneur.

Figure 1.3 – Business Plan Compass

Triad = Passion, Talent, Opportunity
Task Inventory Exercise—Passion (P):

1. List all the work and social tasks you are responsible for today.
2. Review the list and highlight the tasks that excite you the most.
3. Rank each highlighted task from 1 to 10, from highest being (1) to lowest being (10).
4. Take the three top-ranked tasks and write them down in a statement that starts with the phrase "I am passionate about ..."

When you complete this task inventory list you will have constructed the first piece of your BPC. Hold onto the complete list and passion statement you created for this exercise, because you will refer back to them again by the end of this chapter to add the next portion of your BPC Triad.

Talent (T):

Your natural talents are the things you do very well with little to no effort; they cannot be acquired like a skill or knowledge. Talent is internal but demonstrated externally for others to perceive or experience. When you inventory the talents you possess and channel them in a positive way, you can create exceptional personal power.

Take, for instance, the athletic abilities of Michael Jordan on the basketball court or the musical creativity of Mozart. How bizarre would it have been if they had decided to deny their natural talents? Imagine Michael Jordan as a hardworking investment broker on Wall Street or Mozart as a common carpenter. We would never have experienced the thrill of watching Jordan's fade-away jump shot against the Utah Jazz to seal the NBA championship. We would never have had the pleasure of listening to Mozart's Symphony no. 40 in G Minor. It is unimaginable to think that these two unforgettable examples of mastery and excellence would never have happened—one an event that took only seconds, and the other a piece of musical brilliance enjoyed for years to come.

If you are not using your finest talents every day

in your profession, it is possible that your moment of mastery or creation of excellence will never happen. At some point during our adolescence, many of us listened to a lecture that went something like this: go to school, get an education, grow up, get a good job, and live a good life working . Depending on your background, the lecture may have included specifics about a college education, recommended professions, marriage, children, and a certain lifestyle. Conveniently for corporate America, this is a good set-up for you to become a dedicated, dependent employee—an employee who will forgo the PLE we outlined in Chapter One. It is clear why so many of us now find ourselves working a job that does not help us solve for SA + FW = PL. The time has come for you to forget that old lecture and to start transitioning now.

You have already crafted your passion statement, so let's complete your **task inventory exercise for talent (T)** using the list you have already created in the first exercise for Passion (P). Take the same list and complete the following steps in this next exercise.

Task Inventory Exercise—Talent (T):

1. Highlight the tasks on the list that you do exceptionally well (better than most of your peers).

2. Rank from 1 to 10 each highlighted task according to your strength of talent, with 1 being the highest.
3. Take the three top-ranked tasks and write them down as your next list.

After you complete this list, you will have assembled the information you need to construct the second portion of your BPC Triad. Your top-ranked tasks will illuminate your talents, which are more obvious and therefore easier to assess by others than your passions. As a result, you will need some help with this exercise.

Again, take your list and call upon two trusted advocates to help you review your talents. It would be best to select people with whom you have worked or partnered in a business or social service capacity. Ask for their feedback on what you have selected as the tasks you've done best and your finest accomplishments. Through this discussion, decide where your talents lie, synthesizing those talents into a few words. Then write down your top talents in a statement directly beneath your passion statement, beginning with the phrase "My talents are …"

The two statements you have written will be revisited again the next chapter, so keep them handy. Understanding your passion and acknowledging your talents are essential for you to transition. They will help you make the choice you have not allowed yourself to make as an employee. Passion and talent are two-thirds of your BPC Triad. In the next chapter we will complete the last piece to the BPC concept.

Step Three
Center of Gravity

The final portion of your BPC Triad is the best opportunity (O) for business. This completes the navigational tool you'll need as a transition entrepreneur. The PLE defines why you should become a transition entrepreneur to create your own personal legacy. By discovering your passion and talents, you have put yourself in an excellent position to connect the last portion of your BPC: the opportunities available in your industry of choice. This is where you pull it all together within the center of gravity in the powerful form of a spinning triad. The triad symbol is the connection between three elements converging into one central point the "sweet spot". It represents you pulling together the forces of your passion, talents and business opportunity. By putting this into motion you will accelerate your personal growth as you build a new business. You now know what you are truly passionate about; you also know what your talents are. Now you need to know the business those passions and talents are best suited for and what direction you should take in terms of industry opportunity. The BPC will show you where you should go to pursue your journey as a transition entrepreneur. You already have the benefits of being an employee; now you want much more.

The Sweet Spot

Do you like where you work today? Your work environment has a major impact upon how well and productively you work. Let's explore some scenarios that may describe your work environment:

You may be sitting in a tidy cubicle or office space staring at a computer all day. Possibly you are standing at a counter, serving clients, or walking a lobby, sales floor, production floor, or department to engage customers. Whatever your current work environment, it is now time for you to choose one that will allow you to explore your passions and talents. This will be the final element the best business opportunity to help you arrive at your "sweet spot"

How you function on the job is usually a direct effect of your work environment. Some people work in large office buildings or spaces with lots of people traffic. Others may work in isolated offices with controlled entry. Still others work from the comfort of a home office. Each environment helps determine how an individual comes into contact with co-workers and the way in which he or she contributes as an employee. How and where you prefer to work can tell you a lot about your preferred work style. Start thinking about your work environment and function today. This will help you understand whether your passions and talents are more suitable for an individual contributor or a group contributor.

Many employees today are frustrated in their jobs simply because they work in an environment and or at a job that does not suit their passion and talents—but they don't recognize the source of their frustration. Case in point: someone with no passion for routine service tasks and no talent for building rapport through conversation would probably dislike working at a call center. An employee in this situation most likely is working just for the paycheck and is liable to quit the job the moment something better comes along.

As a transition entrepreneur, you get to determine the best job and work environment for you. You also get to determine whether or not you will be an individual or group contributor. Take off your employee hat and put on your new hat as a transition entrepreneur. Here is your golden moment to be who and what you want to be.

Let's tie the PLE concept to the BPC concept by defining the final element of your triad. You wish to become a transition entrepreneur in order to create your own personal legacy, thus solving for the PLE equation: achieving self-actualization + maximizing financial wealth. The way toward achieving this goal is by defining your passions, your talents, and your best opportunity to build your own business, the variables that comprise your BPC. Having considered your work environment, and preferred work style, you now have a basis for drafting your opportunity statement.

In your notepad or journal, write a statement describing your preferred work environment and work style that best emphasize your passion and talents. The statement should be formatted as such: "My preferred work environment is …"; "I function best by working with …"; and "The best way for me to be productive is … (choose either *individual* or *group* contributor)."

Now that we have addressed work environment and preferred work style, we can move on to the topic of business opportunities, which we can identify by establishing some fundamental business principles. We will start by breaking down the major forms of industry and some examples of industry segments. You will use your prior work on the task inventory exercises (P) and (T) along with the three statements in your notebook or journal to narrow down your focus. We will refer to a sample BPC example of John Doe an auto mechanic as a point of reference for you to leverage in building your business plan. At the end of this chapter you will be ready to start your career bridge.

Industry 101

There are four common classifications of industry. It's important to recognize that each of these industries is now interdependent and global as a result of advances in technology and distribution. Here are the four industry segments and the major players within each:

- **Agriculture:** farmers and miners growing or extracting commodities and unfinished raw materials for manufacture
- **Manufacturing:** builders and manufacturers of products developed from grown or raw materials into finished products
- **Service:** those who service, sell, or distribute finished manufactured products for consumption, or intangible services for use
- **Intellectual (Development/Technology):** highly skilled, certified, or licensed professionals providing services that are specialized or technologically advanced

Determine which industry you work in today as an employee. As a developing transition entrepreneur, you will need to decide which industry is a good match for you passion and talents, and which gives you the best opportunity to be most productive in terms of work environment and function. Keep in mind that you have already done the hard part by completing the two exercises in Chapter Two, the task inventory exercises (P) and (T) that helped you draft all three statements of your BPC. Without these preliminary steps, selecting a preferred industry might feel like looking for a penny in the Atlantic Ocean.

Pick up the notebook or journal where you have written about your passion, talents, and opportunity; read all three statements aloud, and then consider which industries would give you the most probability of creating your own legacy (PLE). Make this a boundless thought process; explore your options by relying on your id (pleasure principle = pleasure and no pain). Imagine you are a child again—full of imagination, but with all your accumulated knowledge, wisdom, and education. Envision yourself standing in front of your class as your teacher asks, "What do you want to do when you grow up?" Let go of all your inhibitions and pick one or two industries you think will give you the bandwidth to exert your passion and talents.

It's very likely that you are currently working in one of your selected industries of opportunity. These industries will become your research project in an upcoming chapter. That research will enlighten and empower you as you drill down within your industry of choice, working systematically to identify a field, market, and product or service to meet a specific customer demand.

You have just completed your business plan compass, creating a center of gravity with the triad of passion, talent, and opportunity. Your BPC is going to help you avoid making one of the most common mistakes of some overzealous entrepreneurs. As a transition entrepreneur, you will not be jumping into a business venture cold turkey, putting yourself at risk with an over-the-top, one-dimensional quest: to get rich overnight, become famous in a day, or seize the power of the world in your hands. Instead, you will put into action the concepts of this book, concepts that are individualized for you and supported by a meticulous and meaningful method for building your business. In the end, you will choose a profitable line of business that allows you to do what you love and what you are good at and to solve for PLE.

Sample Business Plan Compass (BPC) Profile:

- Employee: John Doe, aged thirty

- Employment: auto body repair specialist
- Employer: ACME Auto Body Shop
- Annual Income: $35,000
- Field Work Experience: eight years

Task Inventory List (P) Top Results:

1. Building, repairing, and restoring automobiles
2. Training and developing auto mechanic apprentices
3. Helping and mentoring auto enthusiasts

Passion Statement:

I am passionate about restoring automobiles.

Task Inventory List (T) Top Results:

1. Auto body work and engine reconstruction
2. Solving challenging mechanical technology problems
3. Creating an inclusive work environment for creative thinkers

Talent Statement:

My talents are reconstructing cars and resolving mechanical problems.

Opportunity Statement:

I work best in an environment with others, I function best when I have multiple ongoing projects, and I prefer to work as a group contributor.

John has completed the task inventory exercises (P) and (T) to draft his passion, talent, and opportunity statements, and he has decided that there are two industry opportunities for him to consider. He is interested in starting a business of his own in auto repair, within the service industry, or in automobile research development, within the intellectual industry. With his passion and talent, pursuing one of these opportunities could help John solve for his PLE. He now has his BPC to help him navigate his research and begin the next stage of his development as a transition entrepreneur.

Use John Doe's BPC to evaluate the plan you have drafted. Note that this BPC is fictitious, and just an example; you should by no means infer that you need to stay within your existing field or profession to become a successful transition entrepreneur. In some cases, your passion and talents may point toward an opportunity in an entirely new industry. Each BPC Triad represents the individual as a unique navigational tool.

It is essential that you fully understand this concept to create a solid BPC, because it will provide direction for the remaining work you will do in this book. The transition is the hardest part of the process, requiring you to reach toward higher self-actualization, as described in Chapter One.

CREATE YOUR BRIDGE

"If you want to succeed you should strike out on new paths, rather than travel the worn paths of accepted success."

John D. Rockefeller

Step Four
Business Research

The BPC you have created is your triad of passion, talent, and opportunity; it will help you navigate your business research. Your passion and talents exercises have simplified the process of identifying your best opportunity to be productive. Now that you have uncovered that opportunity, you can determine which specific industry is a match for you by researching the hard business facts. You also need to ensure that the business opportunity you choose is one that will provide you real financial gain beyond the intrinsic value of achieving self-actualization. Remember the entrepreneur's adage: Either you are in business for profit, or you are simply in a hobby.

Macro View

We will start by taking a macro view of the industries of interest you identified in the last chapter, researching data related to three macroeconomic variables: (1) the gross domestic product (GDP), the country's total annual productive output; (2) the unemployment rate report, the status of national/state laborers seeking employment; and (3) the inflation rate, this rate is an indicator of the relative prices of common goods and services.

This high-level view can help you gauge overall economic conditions and the opportunities for entry into your industry of choice. These variables help you view the landscape of all industries before you begin drilling down to a more specific level; you must explore the current trends in labor productivity and any changes in the unemployment rate to get a real grasp of the demand for the product or services you are considering. Start by accessing the U.S. Bureau of Labor Statistics website, www.bls.gov, and following these steps:

1. Click the title tab **Economic Releases** and then select **Major Economic Indicators**.
2. This will bring you to a page with a list of **report links.**
3. You will want to review two monthly reports:

the **Consumer Price Index** and **Real Earnings**.

Next you should review a quarterly report, the Employment Cost Index.

The purpose of reviewing these reports is to provide you an overview understanding of the current economy and specific status of national impact on average consumer households. This will give you a sense of an average Americans' quality of life relative to the cost of common goods. It also will provide an economic status for all industry segments, including consumer demand and business production. It will take some dedicated time to digest this data. Use your journal or notepad to make notes on trends and percentages of change regarding variables like cost of goods, employment expenses for businesses, and growth in output. Then you can refer back to your notes as you drill down to your specific industry of interest.

Micro View

Now that you have attained a greater base of knowledge through macro research, the next step is to uncover the core information you are looking for. Again, the U.S. Bureau of Labor Statistics website (www.bls.gov) is your best source for information.

Here are the next steps to follow, focusing on your specific industry of interest:

1. Click the tab titled **Subject Areas**. The subjects you will review are **Spending Time & Use, Employment,** and **Productivity**.

2. Under **Spending Time & Use,** review the **Consumer Expenditures Survey** to get data on average household expenses in your industry as a percentage of total disposable income. Pull the report table titled **Composition of Consumer Unit** to see units demanded, by segment, in various industry lines: food, housing, apparel, transportation, health care, entertainment, education, etc. Next pull the **American Time Use Survey** to see how consumers use their work and leisure time, by category. This data will be helpful as you draft your business plan later, so document it in your journal.

3. Under **Employment**, click on **Labor Force Statistics** from the **Current Population Survey**. This will direct you to review the **Employment Situation Survey** report, which provides employment data for your selected industry. This includes important information about demographics, typical

compensation, and employment risks that you will need to consider for your business plan. Pay close attention to long-term trends to determine whether opportunities for businesses entering the industry are growing or shrinking. Document this data in your journal.

4. Now you will pull data from the **Productivity** area, reviewing **Productivity and Cost by Industry** to get an idea of output trends and changes in your chosen industry. This will help you determine whether that industry is growing or declining before you make the decision to enter it as a transition entrepreneur.

It's important that you gauge the annual sales (demand) for your industry of interest in order to build upon your understanding of labor economics. You can access this information through the website of the U.S. Census Bureau, at factfinder.census.gov. From the main page, under the heading **Fact Finder**, click on **Business and Government** and then select the **Economic Fact Sheet**. The fact sheet lists each industry by North American Industry Code System (NAICS), with a description to list each segment such as food, retail, auto, and jewelry, including the total annual sales/shipment/receipt averages.. This information is important for you to understand the demand within your selected industry, because your goal is to take some of this market share as a new business owner. To the far right of the listings, a link to "more" allows you to further explore specific segments of each industry. Navigate this path to get more information on your area of interest. If you plan to meet consumer demand, it's imperative that you understand the trends in that demand and in the competitive pool.

Now you're ready to make an informed and thoughtful decision. You are armed with important economic information about how current trends in national productivity, the labor market, and price sensitivities might impact the industry you hope to transition into. You need to know how much demand there is for your proposed product or services in order to determine the feasibility of taking on this new venture.

By taking your research further, to the regional and state levels, you will be even better equipped to make wise financial projections in your business plan for first-year annual sales. With all this information, you can do a final self-check using the concepts outlined in this book before moving into the next chapter—building your business brand and creating an actionable, formal business plan.

Step Five
Build Your Business Brand

You know your target customer from your research; the data identified by gender, age, household income, and geography who might buy your product or service. The information also provided you this data by period trends of consumption and time allocation for your area of business enterprise. This will help you avoid the costly mistake made by many overzealous start-up business owners: hedging on a great idea without validating the demand for the new product or service.

Now that you've identified your target demographic, you can make it easier to fulfill customers' demands by building a strong business brand. Customers should be able to recognize your product or service in a nanosecond. For example, whenever you drive or walk the streets of your city and see the golden arches, you think immediately of McDonald's, and I'll bet you can almost taste their french fries, too. Or whenever you see a certain white swoosh, what comes to mind? "Just do it"—and all the great athletes associated with Nike shoes and apparel. These are just two brands that transcend continents, languages, cultures, and gender because the brands are stable, powerful, and easy to identify. Long-standing brands like these do not happen by chance; they are built with precision and intent.

The purpose of your business should be transparent to your target customer, who should easily understand why he or she should consider becoming a loyal consumer of your product or service. This transparency is created by the value representation of your brand. Your business brand must differentiate you from your competition.

In order for you to create a strong, unique brand, you will need to take advantage of some marketing basics, starting with the "four Ps" of marketing: positioning, placement, pricing, and product. Building a brand is complex, but it's vital to creating a strong business identity in a brand-saturated global marketplace, with its viral media, social media forums, and online shopping.

Let's discuss the four Ps using the information gathered from your business research.

Positioning: What is your target market segment in your selected industry? Who is your target customer? Narrow these down to the demographic groups (age, education level, household type, gender) currently demanding what you will produce.

Placement: Where and how will you deliver consistent, quality products or services? How would your target customer like to purchase your product or use your service: at brick-and-mortar locations, online, by telephone, or through a combination of these distribution channels? In this case, the saying "If you build it, they will come" does not apply. You have to go where your customers want or need to buy your product or service.

Pricing: What is the competitive market price for your product or service? At what cost do you need to produce it in order to make a profit? If your price is too high, customers might choose a lower-cost substitute. However, if your price is too low, you could squeeze your profit margin and stall your ability to grow. Pricing is very much like porridge: it should be just right

Product: Make it easy for your customers to recognize the benefits of your product, what's in it for them. The specific design or function features of your product and service should tell your customer why you are different, special, and better than your competition. This should be immediately obvious so that your target customer can make that determination with little effort.

The four Ps and the questions associated with

them will become the DNA of your brand value proposition. They will help you position your product or service and craft the best message for all marketing, advertisements, special offerings, presentations, and other communications.

For example, imagine you are selling monogrammed leather briefcases to a target demographic of college-educated working professionals aged twenty-five to forty-five, living in households earning more than fifty-thousand dollars a year. You need to position, place, and price your product in a manner that makes it readily accessible to that target customer, offering benefits compatible with his or her interests or desires.

Write the answers to the four P questions in your journal, because they will be essential to your business plan. After you have developed a business brand, compare it to some of your favorite brands by searching them on the Web. When you pull up their websites, answer the same four P questions. Review the website to identify specific product design features and benefits in the company page messages, photos and trademark slogans. Reflect upon which features or benefits you find most appealing about the product. This should be a fun exercise that will give you some perspective on how the company branding has positively impacted you as a customer. Try to narrow down which features and benefits most influenced your buying decision. You will want the features and benefits of your product to influence your target customers to choose your product over similar alternatives. This is important thought processing that is going to help you build your own business brand.

Now you can use the proven methodology of a formal business plan to transform the work you've done thus far into the business you deserve as transition entrepreneur.

Step Six
Network Marketing Plan

Circle of Influence

Test your brand within your close circle of influence—your friends, family, colleagues, and trusted advisors. They will help you measure the quality of your product value proposition, set your pricing, challenge your positioning, and determine effective placement. Word of mouth and the direct-sampling approach are the most cost-effective ways to create a network of potential customers for your new business. Here are just a few proven methods to consider:

- Host a product launch gathering or party to create buzz about your new company.

- Post trademark-protected images of your company or product on social network forums.
- Provide close friends, family, and associates with free samples of your product or service to get feedback on its benefits and features.
- Participate in relative newsgroups discussion forums; use blogs and speaking forums to spread the word about your business.
- Join associations and affiliations in your industry to make new contacts for future partnerships or sponsorships.

Test and Learn

The feedback you get from networking about your product will provide insight into the best way to distribute it and which customer segment to target first. Keep in mind that, initially, you will be making a large investment in time and capital with a low return on that investment. You'll learn more about the market and the demand for your product from the networking interactions among your circle of influence. They will help you learn invaluable lessons about opportunities to establish your business by providing you feedback and possibly new ideas.

A great way to synthesize information from prospective customers and contacts in your network is with online surveys. There are many tools available online with step-by-step instructions for creating a survey. As you collect contacts via business cards, social media, and news groups discussion forums, follow up with them by sending out a survey to learn their preferences related to your product or service. Then try to pinpoint the top benefits and positive features that are a reoccurring theme among your customers and contacts. This is what future customers likely will demand, and so this is where you should focus your brand to best position the product or service you offer.

Reinforce Your Brand

Now that you have taken advantage of real customer feedback to refine your product value, work on reinforcing and deepening your brand as an enhanced marketing strategy. For example, using the briefcase scenario from the last chapter, imagine that the majority of customers who received a free prototype briefcase all agreed on three core benefits or features of the product:

- The shoulder straps are comfortable.
- The leather is soft and attractive.
- The inner zip pockets are convenient for storage.

With this insight from potential customers, we can maximize our market penetration by enhancing these benefits and features during product development. We should also ensure that the buying customer can easily notice these features compared to other, similar products on the market. Our sales and service representatives would be trained to focus on these benefits as selling points and demonstrate full knowledge of the product's features.

As the business's founder, you will be responsible for branding the product or service at every given opportunity to highlight the key features your target customer demands. Think about how often you see or hear brand reinforcement on television, the radio, and the Internet, in the newspapers, and on coupons and billboards. Coke is a perfect example of masterful brand reinforcement; the Coca-Cola Company consistently reinforces its position as the premier choice for soda refreshment. Coke reinforces this theme without even using the word *refreshment*, simply by showing someone drinking the beverage, sighing, and smiling in relief. Coke wants to be known as the ubiquitous refreshment; therefore it is distributed everywhere, for everyone to enjoy.

In order to be like the best, you have to reinforce like the best. Over time, deepen your brand penetration in the places where your customers are most likely to purchase your product or be exposed to your primary competitors' products. You will need to work very hard to dominate the minds and hearts of your primary customers so it becomes their first instinct to seek out your product or service.

In today's competitive world, with so many product offerings representing so many benefits, branding is everything. Do not allow yourself to get trapped into trying to be everything to everyone. Your brand should be well-defined; stay true to your target customer. Note that Coca-Cola does not attempt to mimic Mountain Dew's extravagant efforts to equate their beverage with excitement and daredevil acts. Think about it: when was the last time you saw a Mountain Dew-type commercial produced by Coca-Cola? Chances are you have never seen or heard any advertisement for Coke that crosses that line. Therefore I am branding the message (pun intended): stick to your brand, and make it simple for your customers.

The Transition

"Be the change that you want to see in the world."

Mohandas Gandhi

Step Seven
Business Plan Format

The business plan you will build using the formal steps outlined below will become a dynamic operating guide for all the decisions you make moving forward.

Executive Summary: Although this will be the first section of your business plan, write it last, after you have completed the entire plan. The executive summary will tell all interested parties, investors, and partners the purpose and scope of your business. The preceding chapters and exercises will help you write this section.

Business Description: This section defines your entity type (sole proprietorship/partnership/corporation), business function (retailer/servicer/manufacturer), and operations (storefront/online). Complete this section second-to-last.

Industry & Market Analysis: We have taken the unconventional but convenient step of doing this research up front, during your business plan compass element tasks and business research for Chapters Three and Four.

Competition: You will need to do first-hand research by assessing local businesses in your field. You can accomplish this by interviewing your competitors and researching similar businesses online. You might even need to purchase or sample your competitors' products to fully assess what you are competing against.

Marketing & Sales Plan: This portion of your business plan will define how you will convey information about your product or service to your primary customer. It will include the forms of marketing collateral items like print advertisements, from the Internet to all channels through which you will create awareness about your product. You did most of the work for this in Chapters Five and Six.

Operations & Technology Plan: Here you will present information on vendors, suppliers, and partners that will help you manufacture, finish, and distribute your product or service. This should include specifics about your operation of any brick-and-mortar location, website, or telecommunications for delivering your finished product or service. By researching your competitors, you can get a great deal of information about the logistics of production and where you can make cost-effective adjustments in the production process.

Leadership Formation & Strategy: The type of business entity will have an impact on how you form your leadership organization. Your leadership and organizational format of ownership or officers should direct how you make business decisions, communicate to the public, handle public relations or legal issues, and strategically grow the business.

Financial & Investment Strategy: The operations and technology cost information above is essential for you to project future profits. You will need financial estimates for required start-up capital, fixed operating costs, tax liabilities, insurance costs, and annual revenue projections. Consult with a good certified public accountant, a business banker, and an attorney to put together a strong financial plan, combining that information with what you will learn in in Chapter Eight.

Appendices: These should include supplemental information such as brochures, résumés for key leaders in your organization, and supporting information such as contracts and photos of your business location.

You can complete this business plan by using the easy-to-follow template provided on the Small Business Administration website, www.sba.gov/busplantemplate/BizPlanStart.cfm.

Step Eight
Investment Strategy

Personal Investment

The obvious and difficult first step in your investment strategy for becoming a transition entrepreneur is putting your money where your mind and heart are. The initial seed money invested in your business will come from you. The majority of the time invested in your business will come from your leisure time. Let me repeat: the important word is *you*. You cannot expect anyone else to invest in your business if you are not willing to invest your own hard-earned dollars and precious time first.

As you take this critical first step, think about how much money and time you spend on entertainment, recreation, and luxury services. How does the return on that investment compare to the potential return on investment in your business? Remember, this is your journey from employee to business owner and entrepreneur. It's a difficult transition that requires you to think differently than you would as a working class citizen simply earning a buck to spend.

Take a close look at your household budget. How much money are you setting aside every month for savings? How much of that money could you invest in your business instead? Exactly how much are you spending on discretionary expenses like dining out, movie tickets/DVD rentals, clothing, travel, and big-ticket purchases? Use your journal or notepad to do the calculations and make a written commitment indicating how much of that money you are going to redirect over the next twelve months to make your dream of entrepreneurship come true. Then keep track of the money you are putting into the business, preferably by using business-specific checks or debit card transactions that will be reflected on your monthly bank statement. This will make it easier for your accountant, banker, and attorney to assist you with financial management, including tax preparation.

Financial Options

Besides your personal investment of disposal income, other conventional forms of start-up financing include loans, grants, sponsorships, and venture capital. We will touch on each option, followed by some guidance about what to expect as you pursue each resource.

Loans: Most start-up businesses can expect banks to ask for more than two years of operation and financial documents demonstrating profitability (recorded on tax returns) before they will consider offering a business loan. Therefore a start-up business requesting a loan will need to provide strong projections that would convince a lender to approve a request. Newer and expanding businesses that have already demonstrated some profitability will often take out a Small Business Administration (SBA) loan in order to expand and accelerate growth. Expanding businesses typically request loans to make capital investments such as purchasing of new equipment, increasing inventory volume and upgrading technology. The SBA loan program is government supported and requires prudence and preparedness in the application process. Before you get too excited about applying, make sure you do your homework and meet with an experienced banker.

The SBA has loan programs that address the financial needs of diverse business types; pay close attention to the Small Loan Advantage & Community Advantage 7(a) Loan Initiatives, which are geared toward helping entrepreneurs, especially those from underrepresented segments of the population. SBA loan opportunities range from special programs to micro-loans and large loans with long-term financing commitments. If you take this route, exercise due diligence by learning what it takes to get ready for approval, and then allow an expert banker to do the processing for you. To learn about the variety of Small Business Administration loans, visit www.sba.gov/category/navigation-structure/loans-grants/small-business-loans/sba-loan-programs.

In some cases, a new business can secure a line of credit or a credit card within the first six months to year of operation, depending upon the principal owner's income and credit worthiness. (The principal owner maintains 20 percent or more of equity in the business.) Of course, personal loans from family and friends can help you avoid having to go through a bank loan process early on. Keep in mind, however, that mixing business with family or friends can be a slippery slope that ultimately is more costly than beneficial, so tread cautiously.

Grants: The United States government offers grants directed to specific businesses whose work impacts one of the following eleven federal entities: the Departments of Education (ED), Agriculture (USDA), Commerce (DOC), Defense (DOD), Energy (DOE), Health and Human Services (DHHS), Homeland Security (DHS), and Transportation (DOT); the Environmental Protection Agency (EPA); the National Aeronautics and Space Administration (NASA); and the National Science Foundation (NSF). To qualify for one of these grants, your business must meet strict guidelines and requirements to show that the scope of your work lies within a particular area of business. Generally, this is an unlikely option for small business owners outside of a very specialized group of transition entrepreneurs in the intellectual/technology industry.

Sponsorships: Some entrepreneurs will ask other businesses to sponsor an event or an ongoing program to cover the start-up's operating costs. In return, the sponsor receives brand recognition, special acknowledgement, and sometimes creative input in the production of the event or program. This funding option can be very effective depending upon your business type, your brand, and your willingness to share power with other players.

Venture Capital: This is the most complex and difficult funding option, because most venture capitalists look for a double-digit return on investment within a very short time frame—one to two years, in most cases. This option is rarely open to small or new businesses simply because you have to be on the cusp of a groundbreaking business opportunity (like Facebook, which from the outset attracted a massive demand) to get the attention of a reputable venture capitalist or firm.

It is vital that you research and wisely consider all financial options relevant to your business type.

Case in point: if you are going to be an entertainment promoter, you may solicit sponsors to underwrite your events; therefore your network of contacts, your reputation, and your experience will be critical to those considering you for a sponsorship. Businesses that offer sponsorships have stiff requirements driven by company standards, and their request process may require application months in advance for an applicant to qualify for limited dollars allocated from annual sponsorship budgets.

Remember that whatever funding option or combination of options you choose, starting your business will also require your personal money and time. It will only happen if you take action to go after the dollars to build your business.

You have already determined in your business plan how much money you need for start-up capital, operating capital to cover monthly expenses . Those financial projections and calculations need to be transparent in your business plan so that your lenders or sponsors or a potential venture capitalist can see how their money will make a difference. This demonstrates that you are serious about your business and that you know how to run a profitable business worth investing in.

Step Nine
Initiate the Business

What sort of business entity will you form as a transition entrepreneur? Before you file with your secretary of state, determine exactly what type of business you wish to launch.

Different types of businesses involve different levels of complexity in terms of formation, legal requirements, tax implications, and permits and licenses.

Discuss these subjects with your accountant, banker, and attorney, and ask them to help you determine the best option for you. For example, if you are planning to sell retail online from home, an accountant can advise you on dealing with sales taxes across state lines. An attorney who is knowledgeable about global e-commerce and a banker who can help you set up a system to accept online credit card payments will be important, too.

Give careful consideration to the type of business entity you choose. If you are going to do all product development, design, and production from your home, for example, it may help to form as a limited liability company (LLC) to reduce your personal risk. Don't simply guess on an entity or select one independently. Instead, consult with qualified experts to help you make the best decision before you open up shop.

Business Formation

The type of business entity you launch—sole proprietorship, partnership, LLC, or corporation—will depend on your chosen industry and market segment. At this point you have the essential information to for your business plan.. Next you will need to consult with a few experts for some sound advice. Before you take that step, let's briefly define the four basic business entities:

Sole Proprietorship: a single owner/operator with no distinction between the individual and the business

Partnership: an agreement between multiple parties to function as a business for their mutual interest

Limited Liability Company: a business of

partners whose liability is limited relative to that of the company itself

Corporation (S or C): a business entity legally recognized by the state as organized by articles of incorporation

The first expert you consult should be a certified public accountant (CPA) with experience in your chosen industry. If you do not already have a relationship with a CPA, ask for a few referrals from your local banker or trusted business advisors. Review your business plan with the CPA and ask what type of business entity you should consider pursuing. Find out what it would cost for him or her to help you get your business filed with the secretary of state. Get quotes from more than one CPA, and compare their quotes to what it would cost to go through a reputable online provider who could help you with the same process. The more money you can save, the better, but you want the job done correctly to prevent future problems with your business operations.

Business Liability

The moment you go into business for yourself, you need to start thinking about the risks associated with being a business owner. As a transition entrepreneur, you have a dual role as both an employee and an owner. Immediately after you receive notification of approved filing with the secretary of state, it would be prudent to consult with an attorney who specializes in your industry. He or she can advise you on legal business protections like copyrights, patents, and trademarks. There are many people in business who could have a negative intent toward or impact on your business without your knowledge. Appropriate preventive measures can help you stay out of court later and secure your rights to all your intellectual and creative products.

Business Services

After you identify a reliable CPA and attorney, begin building a relationship with a trusted business banker and insurance agent. The sooner you establish a bank checking account in the name of your business, the better. Most banks want to help you grow from the start, and they will determine your readiness for credit extension and assess you as a credit risk based upon your strong history of deposits. It often takes up to two years of profitable business operations (verifiable by financial documents like tax returns) and a two-year relationship at the bank before you can get approved for a loan or a line of credit. Therefore, start early and strong in building the financial reputation of your business. That's not only good for business; it's also good for business expansion if you need help with capital expenditures or cash-flow support.

Business insurance coverage is another important service you may need initially, depending upon your business type and operating location. If you are operating out of your home, your home insurance policy might offer an additional policy rider to cover your business equipment and operations in the case of loss or damage.

Permit & Licenses

Some businesses are required by state or federal law to hold specific permits or licenses. Here is a quick list of businesses that fall into that category:

- Barbers and beauty salons
- Child care service providers
- Construction contractors
- Debt collection agencies
- Electricians
- Home health providers
- Massage therapists
- Money service businesses (ex. Check cashing businesses)
- Plumbers
- Real estate appraisers and agents
- Restaurants

The Small Business Administration website (www.sba.gov) again can provide you with all relevant state and federal requirements.

The appropriate licenses and permits will keep you in business for the long term. Don't cut corners on this for the short-sighted view of saving money or time; you may never recover from the financial liability and damage to your reputation that can result from not having the right credentials. Even if getting the required certifications delays the execution of your business plan, it will be well worth the wait to do business the right way.

Executing Your Business Plan

You have done the important work of self-reflection, research, planning, and investing. You are now on the ninth and final step toward making your dream a reality. As a transition entrepreneur, you are about to enjoy the first return on your investment: the emotional and personal reward of solving the the Personal Legacy Equation with the end solution of creating a business. The work you have done has unlocked your full potential and revealed to you a new source of financial possibilities for achieving that potential. You've identified your passion, your talents, and your best opportunity to be productive as a transition entrepreneur. You are on a course for success because you have constructed the navigational tool you need: your Business Plan Compass.

The material and tangible returns will come when you execute your business plan using your valuable time and your hard-earned money. The best way to do this is by setting a clear time line with the defined business objectives, detailed tasks, and expected outcomes.

Let's finish where we started and remember why you have come this far. Being an employee is not enough for you, and it does not define you. You want and need more in order to create a personal legacy with purpose and value. Now the only obstacle you have to face is your own potential procrastination. You are going to overcome this by product of fear by outlining the business objectives:

- Proofread your business plan and write the **Executive Summary.** This will give your plan scope and focus for the benefit of all involved parties.
- Meet with your business partner or leadership team to agree on the final draft of your business plan.
- Complete all necessary business filings, certifications, and set-up of services using your business plan.
- Execute the investment strategy of your

- business plan to start acquiring your **start-up capital**.
- Invest that start-up capital following the **Operations & Technology** section of your business plan.
- The initial investment should trigger your set-up of a business office with the necessary equipment and resources to develop a work schedule outside your regular employment hours.
- Initiate the **Marketing & Sales** section of your business plan to create demand for your first product or service.
- Set up a time line indicating when you expect to complete these tasks by making a firm commitment on your planner or electronic calendar.

The success of your journey will become evident by your customers' first purchases and their feedback about your business. The fulfillment you gain as you build your new business will be unlimited. You have made the difficult transition from employee to entrepreneur, and you now are in control of your future.

As a transition entrepreneur, you will see the world differently. You now have the vantage point of knowing what is possible beyond just working to fulfill your obligations as an employee. You can trust that tomorrow you will not call yourself into an office to terminate your employment; that you will fully respect, understand, and appreciate your new boss; and that every dollar you earn will increase your own bottom line. Most important, you will be creating a business that is connected to the best of your passions and talents. And in doing so, you will redefine your purpose, increase your potential, and live your legacy.

Afterword

As a business professional and perpetual student, I realize that education— formal and informal—builds stronger professionals and businesses. By reading this book, you have enhanced your education by formal research of important public information; you've also learned informally by interacting with others as you completed the nine steps in this book.

I hope you feel the same sense of personal pride and emancipation that I experienced going through these steps. The reason I was able to write this book and share these concepts is because I have personally made the successful climb up that staircase, becoming a transition entrepreneur. I had some of the same fears, concerns, and reservations you probably experienced in making this change, but I learned that the process of "becoming" was just as meaningful as the results of making my dream come true.

Today I have a blooming consulting business that has given me more rewards and financial well-being in a short time than I ever could have imagined. Thank you for joining me on this journey and believing in yourself. My life purpose is to help others achieve self-actualization. My intent and hope is that this book will be one of many contributions I make toward that noble purpose.

"Faith is taking the first step even when you don't see the whole staircase."

Dr. Martin Luther King Jr.

About the Author

J.Bilal is president and founder of Marjalles Consulting LLC. He has twenty years' experience working in the American financial industry. He earned his bachelor of arts degree in economics at the University of Minnesota and his master of business Administration at the University of Phoenix, balancing his studies and a demanding career. His intellectual agility and varied talents enabled him to work in six diverse business lines, assuming more than ten leadership roles during his career. He is masterful at harnessing the talents of others and helping them develop critical skills for success. He has mentored scores of clients and friends into career promotions and through difficult career transitions. J.Bilal has an uncanny way of helping others think through business decisions and draw upon their personal strengths; his approach is to ask provocative questions, creating a virtual mirror for others to see in themselves what is possible. Inspired by some of the greatest thinkers, J.Bilal is boundless in his thinking and ability to understand individuals. He is an exceptional leader, highly motivating public speaker, and accomplished life coach.

Marcellus Rainey

www.ingramcontent.com/pod-product-compliance
Lightning Source LLC
Chambersburg PA
CBHW030858180526